ROSALIND KERVEN

HOW DID THE WORLD BEGIN?

Illustrated by
Angela Lumley

OXFORD
UNIVERSITY PRESS

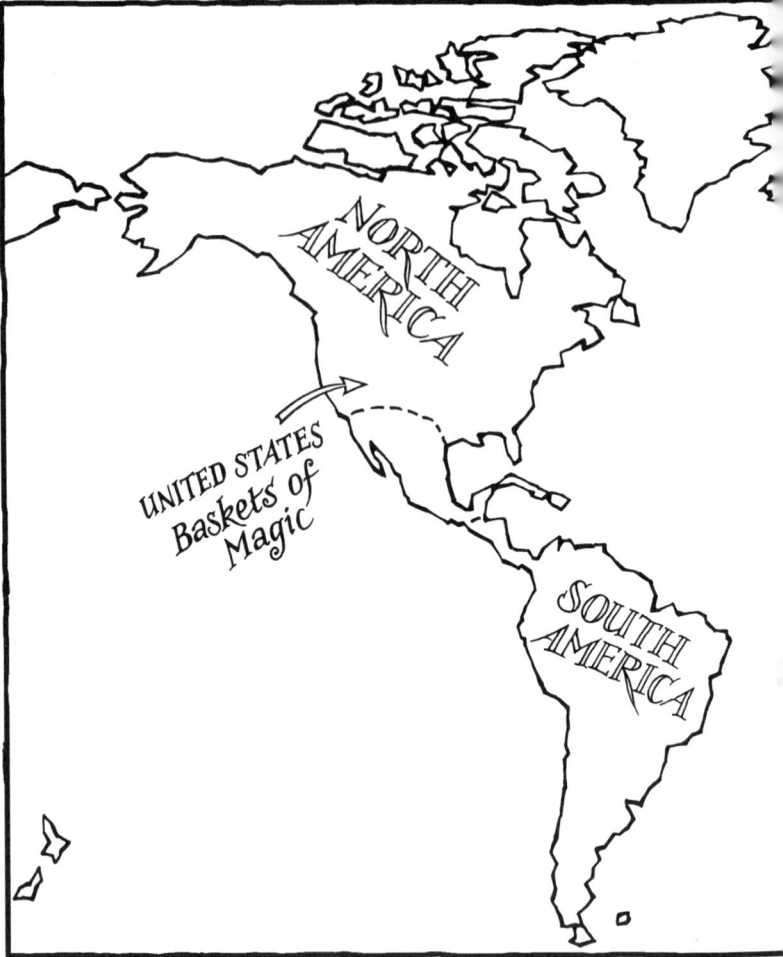

NORTH AMERICA

UNITED STATES
Baskets of Magic

SOUTH AMERICA

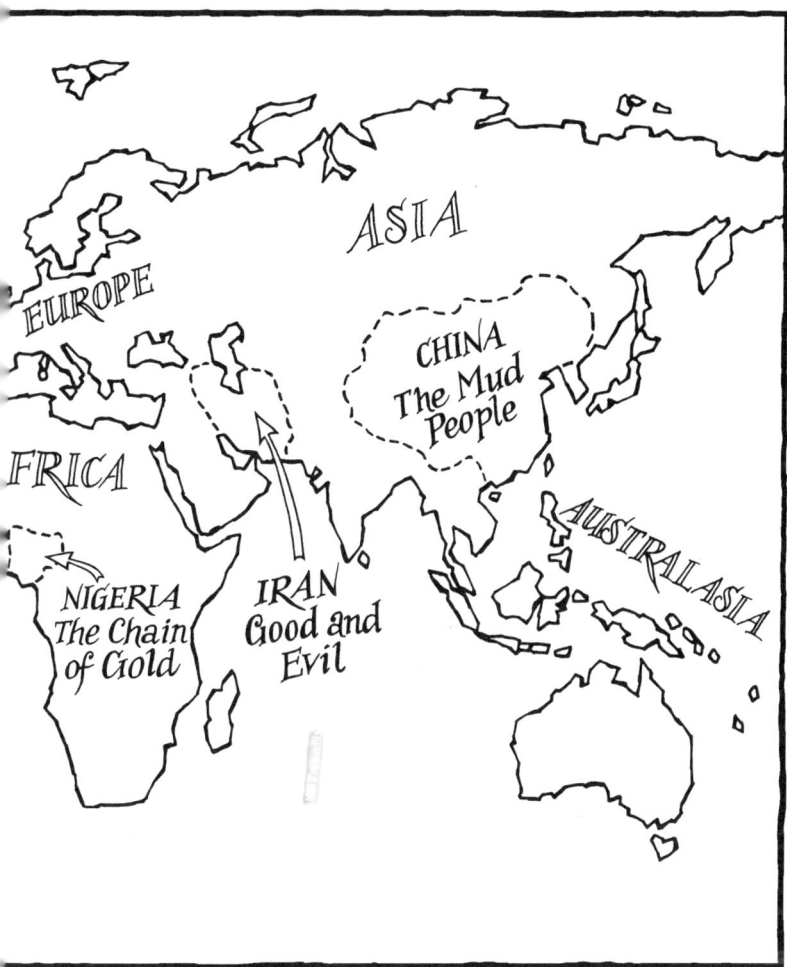

ASIA

EUROPE

AFRICA

NIGERIA
The Chain
of Gold

IRAN
Good and
Evil

CHINA
The Mud
People

AUSTRALASIA

OXFORD

Great Clarendon Street, Oxford OX2 6DP

Oxford University Press is a department of the University of Oxford.
It furthers the University's objective of excellence in research, scholarship,
and education by publishing worldwide in

Oxford New York

Athens Auckland Bangkok Bogotá Buenos Aires Cape Town
Chennai Dar es Salaam Delhi Florence Hong Kong Istanbul Karachi
Kolkata Kuala Lumpur Madrid Melbourne Mexico City Mumbai Nairobi
Paris São Paulo Shanghai Singapore Taipei Tokyo Toronto Warsaw

and associated companies in Berlin Ibadan

Oxford is a trade mark of Oxford University Press
in the UK and in certain other countries

© Oxford University Press 2001
Text © Rosalind Kerven 2001
The moral rights of the author have been asserted
Database right Oxford University Press (maker)
First published 2001

British Library Cataloguing in Publication Data
Data available

ISBN 0 19 915959 9

Printed in the UK by Ebenezer Baylis & Son Ltd

Available in packs

Year 5 / Primary 6 Pack of Six (one of each book) ISBN 0 19 915963 7
Year 5 / Primary 6 Class Pack (six of each book)   ISBN 0 19 915964 5

Contents

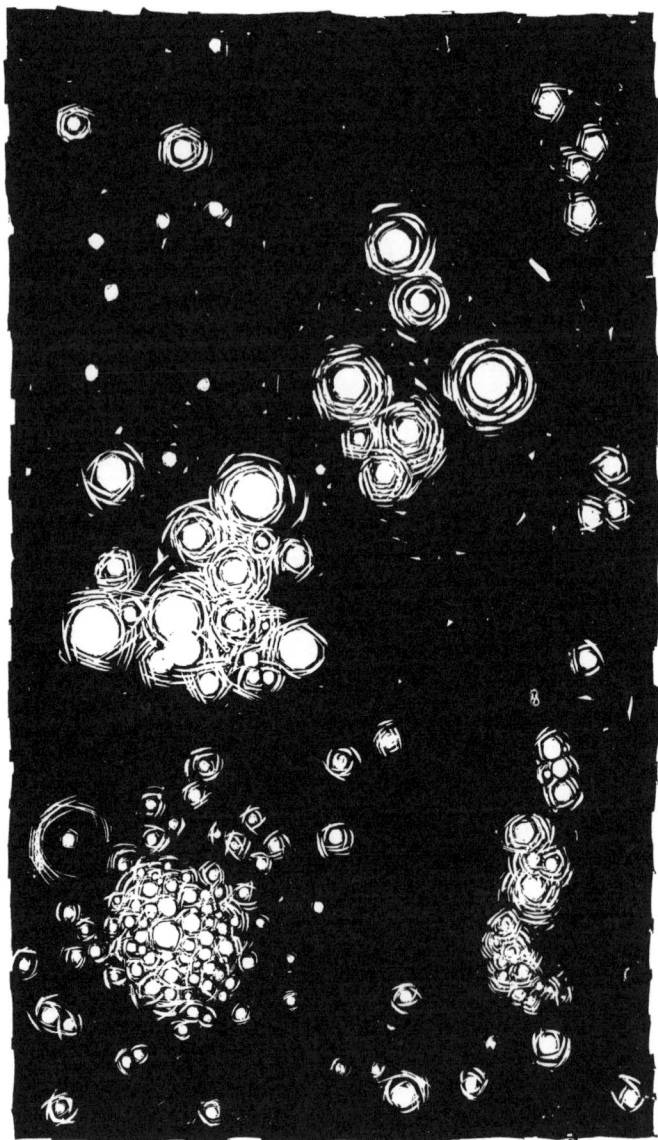

Introduction

Have you ever wondered: where did the first ever people come from? How was the world made? And what was there, what happened, right at the very beginning of time?

Of course, these are extremely difficult questions. Even scientists can only really guess at the answers.

Their experiments and mathematical calculations suggest everything started with a "Big Bang". This was an enormous explosion which formed the universe, including the Earth. Scientists say that the first living creatures came from the sea. These creatures slowly changed over millions of years until some of them became apes and finally humans. Extraordinary! Yet most people today believe this is probably true.

However, long before scientists got to work, people all over the world were asking the same big questions. These people were very deep thinkers. Some had strange dreams or visions in which they seemed to see the answers to their questions. They came up with many different, mysterious theories, which they explained in stories. These stories are known as "creation myths".

A creation myth usually belongs to a religion. Some religious people believe that their own creation myth is really true. Others say that the story is a very simple way of trying to describe something very complicated and difficult.

The creation myths in this book come from four very different cultures. Each one is written in the style of the people to whom the story belongs. Like all myths, they were originally told aloud before they were written down. So when you read each one, try to imagine how it would sound if you were listening to it in a distant country long ago: open your mind to it, and let the strange, shivery magic of an ancient story teller's words wash over you...

Baskets of Magic

A Native American creation myth

Let's go back, right to the beginning. What was there?

Well, there was land. The land has always been here. But we must go below the land, deep, deep under the ground, into the darkness.

Imagine it: thick darkness everywhere. But it was not empty. For within the darkness, two tiny specks were alive and growing. Very, very slowly, these specks took shape. They grew bigger and stronger; they became conscious and began to think. Soon they had become two young girls. They were the very first people!

The girls couldn't see each other, because of the darkness. But they could speak and touch each other. They talked a lot and found friendship and love, like sisters.

They soon found that they were not alone, for a voice came calling to them out of the darkness. "Listen, children!" it said. "I am with you. I will teach you everything you need to know."

At first the girls were frightened of this invisible voice. "Who are you?" they whimpered. "What are you? Are you evil or good?"

The voice answered them gently: "Don't worry! I am called Tsitctinako. I am only a spirit, but I promise to be like a mother to you. You have a lot to learn and a lot to do. That's why I've been sent to you."

"That's all very well," said one of the

girls, "but where did you come from?"

"I've come from the sky," said the spirit. "Your father Utc'tsiti, sent me here."

"But where is the sky? What is it?"

"I can't really describe it," said the spirit, "but I promise you will see the sky for yourselves before long. Then you will understand."

The other girl asked, "Why must we stay here, blindly in the dark?"

"You won't have to stay here for much longer," answered the spirit. "Just be patient until everything is ready. Then you can go out into the wide world where it is light, and you will be able to see. Now, hold out your hands for I want to give you each a gift."

It handed each girl a large basket. These baskets were extremely heavy and rattled curiously when they were shaken, for they were full of many strange things.

The girls both felt inside and let their fingers explore what was there. Some of the things they found were small and hard: they dribbled through their fingers like dry grains of sand.

"Ah," said the spirit, "you have found the seeds. Although right now they seem dead and useless, one day they will transform themselves into amazing things called plants."

The rest of the objects inside the baskets were slightly bigger. They were lumps of solid clay, formed into particular shapes.

"Those are the images of animals, birds, reptiles and fish," said the spirit. "Soon I will tell you how to make them come alive. But for now we must go back to the seeds. Feel inside your baskets again: see if you can find four special ones."

When the girls had succeeded in pulling out the right seeds, the spirit said, "You must bury these in the earth beneath your feet. Then you can go to sleep for a while. When you wake up, you'll have a big surprise."

The two girls put the seeds in the earth, as the spirit had told them. Then they lay down and slept deeply for a long time. When they finally awoke, they were astonished to find that the seeds had grown into four enormous trees!

One of these trees stretched high enough to reach the covering of earth far above them. It had pushed its way through to make a small hole. A fine ray of light was shining down it. This was the very first light the two girls had ever seen. It dazzled their eyes, but they were so excited, they couldn't stop staring at it.

"Hush, hush, stay calm," said the spirit. "There's a lot more to do. Feel inside your baskets again. Which of you has the image of an animal called 'badger'?"

Soon one of the girls found the image that the spirit had described.

"See if you can guess the magic to give it life," said the spirit.

The girl held the image on her hand. She bent over it and whispered, "Come alive!"

At once, it became warm and soft. It grew into a badger's normal size. It breathed. Fur sprouted thickly all over it. It nuzzled the girl then jumped from her hand.

"Go up to the light, friend Badger," said the spirit. "Dig around the hole up there. Make it bigger."

The badger ran up the tree to the hole and began scooping at the mud with its strong front paws. Now the hole was so big that the light shone very strongly through it. When its work was done, the badger came back and lay quietly at the girls' feet.

The spirit praised it. Then it said to the other girl, "Look in your basket for the image of an insect called 'locust'."

Obediently, she pulled the locust out and commanded it to come alive. It spread its wings, flew up to the hole and covered the sides with sticky plaster to make it firm. Then it disappeared through the hole and flew away. The spirit said, "Now the great moment has come: it is time for you to emerge into the world above! Go to the tallest tree and climb up it. Don't stop until you reach the light."

So the two girls went to the tallest tree. They clasped its trunk, feeling the roughness, breathing in its sweet, earthy smell of pine. Then they began to climb it, up and up, all the way to the light-hole far above. The badger followed.

At last they came to the top – and stepped out onto hard, solid ground! They felt the good earth beneath their feet and took long breaths of the clean, pure air. A soft wind played on their faces. They gazed around in wonder, for now they were right out of the darkness and for the first time they could see everything!

Behind them, the great yellow sun was rising in the sky. They felt its warmth on their backs. They turned round to look at it: and at once they screamed for their eyes were burning! They had never dreamed that anything could be so powerfully hot and dazzling.

The spirit Tsitctinako was still with them. "Hush," it said. "Be at peace. Just let your eyes rest for a while. They'll soon get used to the light. Then I can show you everything."

When the girls felt more comfortable Tsitctinako said, "Turn again to the place where you saw the sun rising. This is called the East. Behind you is the West, where each night the sun sinks into sleep. To your left is the North, and to your right is the South. You already know what lies beneath you: the dark earth, where everything begins and ends. Now, look up above you: that is the sky, the place that I told you about. The sky has four layers and your father, Utc'tsiti, lives in the top one. Can you remember all this?

The sisters nodded.

"Then listen some more," said Tsitctinako. "You are different now. You are no longer young girls: you have matured into women. So it's time to learn your names.

"You, on the right are called Ia'tik. Your name means 'Bringing-to-life'. You, on the left, are Nao'tsiti. Your name means 'More-of-everything-in-the-basket'. If you have any questions, ask me."

"Please," said Ia'tik, "can you tell us why we were created?"

"Your father commanded it," said Tsitctinako. "It was he who made everything you can see so far: the world, the sun and the sky. But he wasn't satisfied with this: he felt the world was too empty. So he made you both too, and left you to ripen slowly in the warm, dark womb of the earth. Now you are ready, he wants you to make plants and creatures to fill the world."

Nao'tsiti said, "But how should we make these things?"

"From the objects in your baskets," said the spirit. "I will tell you what to do."

For many hours the two women sat and

listened. The spirit taught them how to pray to their father, and how to sing the great Creation Song so that its echoes would sink into every nook and cranny of the bright new world. By the time it had told them everything, the sun was setting in the west and darkness was falling. The two sisters were dismayed at this, for they thought that all the terrible darkness had been left far behind them under the ground.

"Don't worry," said Tsitctinako, "this is only night time. Soon the light will come back just as brightly as before. That's how things work in the world that your father made."

The two sisters were relieved to hear this. They lay down and slept until the rising sun returned to nudge them awake.

The spirit said, "Now it's time to take all the seeds from your baskets and plant them."

They found that there were hundreds

and thousands of different seeds. They threw them out to the wind, scattering them far and wide. Days and nights passed. Sometimes it rained. The seeds grew into shoots and then into green plants.

"Come here," the spirit called to them one day. "Do you see this plant? It is called corn. I want you to pick it, then grind its grain, mix it with water, cook it and learn how to eat."

The sisters said, "What is cooking? What is eating? All this is new to us."

"I will teach you," said Tsitctinako.

That night, a storm exploded in the black sky. Lightning flashed, and a fragment of it fell to earth.

"This is fire," the spirit told them. "Feed it with leaves, twigs and branches from the trees you have grown. Then place the mixture of corn grains and water in the fire's warmth: the flames will cook it for you."

They did this. Soon the corn and water were baked and transformed into bread. The sisters split it between them and tasted it. This was the first time they had ever eaten anything.

"I had better warn you," said Tsitctinako. "From now on you will have to eat every day. Your father has sent you food to keep you alive and healthy, and to give you strength. Don't forget to eat regularly, otherwise you'll waste away and die."

The next day the spirit told them, "Time is getting on. Now you must create some other creatures. Each of you, take one of the little clay images from your baskets."

The sisters did this.

"Sing to them," said Tsitctinako.

The sisters sang the Creation Song.

"Say to them, 'come alive!'" said Tsitctinako.

"Come alive!" cried the sisters.

At once the two shapes turned into mice. They jumped from the women's hands and ran off into the sunshine.

Now the women pulled out many other clay images. They sang to them and told them to live. These images turned into rabbits, deer, elk, sheep, buffalo, mountain lions, wolves, wildcats, bears and many other animals. They became eagles, hawks and small birds; fish, snakes and turtles. That's how there are so many different kinds of creature in our beautiful world.

The sisters also found some stones in their baskets. They hurled them out, north, south, east, and west. Where the stones fell to earth, they became mountains.

At last all the creation work was finished. The two women were sad about this. They felt tired and restless, and so they began to quarrel.

Ia'tik said, "I'm the eldest. I'm better than you."

Nao'tsiti answered, "You're lying! You know we were both created at exactly the same time. Why should I let you get the better of me?"

All day long they argued and watched each other suspiciously. They both became very unhappy.

A snake saw this with its yellow eyes. It called Nao'tsiti to crouch by it in the dark shadow of a rock.

"You would be better off away from your sister," it hissed. "Find other companions instead."

"That's impossible," said Nao'tsiti. "My sister and I are the only people in the world."

"That may be how things are now," hissed the snake, "but the future could be different. You should look to the rainbow for help." Then it slithered quietly away into the ground.

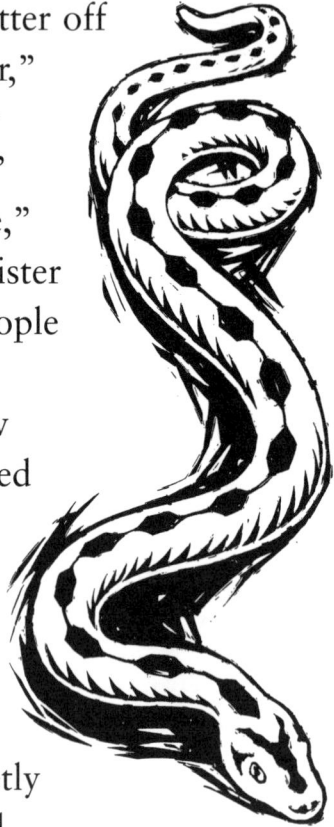

For a long time Nao'tsiti thought about the snake's mysterious words. At last she went away in secret and sat quietly waiting on a rock. Rain fell and the sun shone through it. Suddenly the rainbow arose in a shimmering fan of colours! The rainbow touched Nao'tsiti softly and gave her the gift of a new kind of seed.

This seed was different from the others: it took root inside her and there it slowly grew. After many months it was finished and Nao'tsiti gave birth to two babies.

She kept one child and gave the other to her sister Ia'tik. Now the women were both happy again. They loved having children to look after.

The children ate and grew and learned until they were strong and wise. Time passed. More children were born to them, and still more, until the world became full of people, just as it is today.

About the people who tell this story

The Native Americans (or American Indians) are the original inhabitants of the USA and Canada. They are split between over a hundred different tribes or nations, each with its own name, language, way of life, and religion.

This story comes from the Native American *pueblo* (village) people of Acoma. They live in the state of New Mexico, in the south-west of the USA, where the weather is usually hot and dry. Acoma is almost a thousand years old – one of the oldest villages in the whole of the USA.

The people of Acoma have their own language called Keresan, which they speak as well as English. In the old days they were mainly farmers, but today many of them work in nearby towns. They are also very skilled at craftwork, particularly pottery.

Their houses are still built in long rows in the traditional style: they are made of stone and *adobe* (sun-dried brick) and stand on top if a high mesa (flat-topped hill). In fact the name "Acoma" means "people of the white rock".

Religion is very important to the *pueblo* people. Their beliefs are based on the idea that everyone should live in harmony with nature. They express this through their myths, like this one which shows that all people, plants and animals originally came from the earth. They celebrate many festivals and ceremonies throughout the year.

Good and Evil

A creation myth from the Zoroastrian (Parsee) religion

I can tell you this: there is something even older than Time itself. It is called... Eternity.

Ah, Eternity! No one can understand its mysteries. It has neither a beginning nor an end. It contains everything: light and darkness, hope and despair, life and destruction.

Within Eternity live the two eternal

beings: the good Wise Lord, and the Evil One. Both have always existed; both will continue for ever.

The Wise Lord is called Ahura Mazda or Ohrmazd. His realm is the purity of light. He came from within the shining light to make the angels; and then he created the Universe.

He made the Universe smooth and round, perfect as an egg. In its centre he placed the Earth.

When the Wise Lord first made our beautiful world, he took care to ensure that it was always warm and radiant summer. The cold of winter never touched it, and the darkness of night was never known. For with his own hands he fixed the sun high in the sky, where its golden rays could shine their joy far and wide. Happiness was everywhere.

Then the Wise Lord created the First Bull, a creature of beauty and power.

After the Bull, he made the first human

being, a man called Gayomard. This Gayomard was perfect. He was immortal: his gift was to live for ever. Never would he grow weak or wrinkled, grey or bent or old. Bad thoughts were unknown to him and misery was a word that meant nothing. Oh happy, happy Gayomard!

But wait! Such perfection, such happiness, can never live unchallenged. That is the law of Eternity. For far below, in the foul darkness, the Evil One was lurking. The Evil One saw the beautiful Universe that the Wise Lord had created. He hated it.

For he loved only cruelty and pain, sickness and ugliness, fear and brute force. He nurtured these horrible visions in the damp, airless night-caverns of his realm, feeding them on the bitterness of ice.

Slowly, these visions became solid and took shape. In this way he created the creatures of nightmares: cold-blooded snakes, scorpions with their poison bites, clouds of darting flies carrying disease and filth.

Next, he spun more shadows and shaped the demons, those grotesque imps of darkness. He blew up searing winds of misery to smother happiness. Finally, he invented Death.

When all these things were finished, the Evil One emerged from Eternity and found his way into the Universe. He slithered, silent and sinister as a snake, through a tiny crack in the sky.

Below him he saw the Earth, its blue ocean and green forests pure and sparkling

in the endless morning. Fury arose in the
Evil One's heart like the bubbling fires of a
volcano. He clutched at the monstrous
things he had made and flung them into
the world.

Then there were earthquakes! The smooth Earth crumpled in pain and distorted itself into narrow valleys and towering mountains. The sun itself went hurtling down from the sky, blacking out the brilliance of day and turning it into night.

Without the sun, the endless summer wilted. A wind blew up, making the leaves shrivel and fall. Sleet filled the air and turned into a wild blizzard. The Earth sank into winter.

At these terrible events, the First Bull bellowed its anguish and Gayomard, the Perfect Man, cried out in pain. Fear gripped both man and beast: they trembled and shrank from the shadows with pangs of terror.

Gayomard called out to the Wise Lord, he begged for help; but the only answer that came back to him was the Evil One's hollow laughter.

Lightning seared across the sky and

thunder made the Earth shudder. The Bull and the Man grew weak, haunted by the crazy dance of demons. Disease came to them both, sucking the life from their bodies. They fell to the ground, froze into its cruel covering of ice, drew their last breaths… and died.

Oh, how could the Evil One work such mischief? Where was the Wise Lord and his radiant powers of light?

Take comfort, my friend: he was still there.

When the Wise Lord saw all the monstrous crimes that the Evil One had committed, he set to work again at once.

First he sealed off all the exits from the Universe. Thus the Evil One was trapped, a prisoner, and his laughter turned to helpless rage.

Then the Wise Lord went to the Bull. Gently, he touched the great beast's silent body. From it he took the seed of life and spread it around the earth. In this way he made all the plants and animals.

Then he turned his loving gaze on the Perfect Man. How peacefully he lay there! Gently, the Wise Lord touched him too, and drew from within him a strange plant.

This plant grew and spread its leaves. From them stepped out a man and a woman. They were the father and mother of all children who have since been born into the world.

And so it was: in this way the world began.

In this way too, the world shall continue through twelve thousand long years, until the very end. And though the Evil One will never cease in his endless battle to destroy us, the Wise Lord will always watch over us and keep us safe.

There is no other way it can be.

About the people who tell this story

This myth belongs to a religion called Zoroastrianism or Parseeism. It began in ancient Persia (modern Iran) at least 2,600 years ago. Today about 130,000 people still follow this religion. Most of them live in small communities in Iran and India.

Zoroastrianism teaches that the world contains both good and evil. Each individual is urged to choose to follow the path of goodness. Prayers are usually said in front of a "sacred fire" which represents the Wise Lord, the source of all light and life.

The Chain of Gold
An African creation myth

At first there were only two places: the Sky above and the Water beneath.

The Water was grey, lonely lifeless: nothing lived in it except for one being, the goddess Olokun. But the Sky was a really fine place, for it was the realm of many gods. Olorun was their chief, and he had power over everywhere and everything.

Olorun sat on his chief's stool, looking down at the monotonous expanse of Water stretched out far below him. Beside him, draped in robes of fine white cloth, sat his favourite friend, Obatala. The two gods were talking.

"What a miserable wilderness the Water is!" said Olorun. "And yet think, Obatala: if only there were solid land down there, it would make space for many living creatures."

"As always, master, your words are very wise," said Obatala. "May I make a humble suggestion?"

"Please do," said Olorun

"This is it," said Obatala. "We should transform the Water down there. We should turn it into dry land."

"I like this idea," said Olorun. "I like it a lot. And Obatala – since the idea is yours, I choose you to make it happen."

"Master," said Obatala, "I am greatly honoured. But I'm afraid I cannot work this miracle alone. I need advice and help."

"And you shall have it, my friend," said

Olorun. "Go now to the house of Orunmila, my eldest son. Tell him what we plan, and ask him to seek help from the hidden powers."

Obatala arose and bowed. Then he walked through the paths of the Sky to Orunmila's house. He knocked on the door, stooped and passed into the cool darkness within. The young god greeted him courteously and enquired why he had come. Obatala told him.

"Please sit," said Orunmila. "I must ask you to be patient."

Orunmila went to a shelf and brought from it a wooden tray containing sixteen palm nuts. He scooped up the nuts, then threw them down again into the tray. As the nuts fell, they made

a mysterious pattern. Orunmila crouched over them, noting the shape of their falling and murmuring secretly to himself. Now he became silent, scooped the nuts up, and cast them again. Many times he repeated this ritual while Obatala sat quietly waiting.

At last Orunmila said, "My friend, I have read the signs and many secrets have been revealed to me. Now I can tell you how to go about this task. Go to my father's goldsmith and ask him to make a great chain, long enough to stretch down from the Sky to the Water below. When it is ready, come back to me and I will give you some useful gifts."

Obatala thanked Orunmila and went to see the goldsmith. When he explained that he needed a gold chain long enough to reach the distant Water, the goldsmith shook his head.

"Good sir," he said, "this is not an easy task. It is a long way from the Sky to the

Water. I do not have enough gold in my stores to complete it. I will have to collect some more."

So the goldsmith went round to the houses of all the gods and goddesses in the Sky. He asked them for gifts of gold for Obatala's project. Some gave him gold rings, some gave bracelets or pendants and others donated baskets of glinting golden dust. The smith took all this into his forge, melted it down and worked it into an enormous chain. He made a strong hook to fasten one end of it to the edge of the Sky. Then he called Obatala to admire his handiwork.

Obatala praised the goldsmith generously. Then he went back to Orunmila saying, "Wise one, the golden chain is ready. If you still have gifts to give me, I am ready to accept them."

Orunmila nodded. From the darkness of his house he brought out a giant snail shell and handed it to Obatala. Inside its deep, hollow coils were four things: a bag of soil, a white hen with five toes, a black cat, and a single nut from a palm tree.

Obatala thanked Orunmila. Then he went to the chain and slid down it. It was a long, long way. The other gods watched him from the Sky. At last they saw him far below, dangling from the chain's end, just above the endless Water.

Obatala took the bag of soil from the snail shell and tipped it over the Water. Then he pulled out the five-toed hen. The hen flew down to the soil and scratched it with her five long claws. In this way she spread the soil here and there, far and wide. Now, where once only water had been, there was a great expanse of dry, solid land.

Obatala let go of the chain and jumped down to the ground. It felt good under his feet. He called the place where he had come to land "Ife".

Obatala pulled the palm nut out of the snail shell and planted it. Time passed. The palm nut grew into a tree. The tree grew big and many more nuts sprouted and swelled on its branches. They fell to earth and grew into new trees. Now there was a rich, green forest.

Obatala built a house in the forest. Then he called softly to the black cat that was still hiding in the snail shell. The cat came slinking out. When it saw Obatala, it began to purr and rub itself against his legs. The god stroked the cat and took it into his house. So they made their home together in the forest. For a while nobody disturbed them and they were happy.

Meanwhile, in the Sky, Olorun often looked at the gold chain hanging down. He said to himself, "I wonder how my friend Obatala is getting on." So he called his messenger, the colour-changing lizard called Chameleon, and sent him down the golden chain to find out.

Obatala welcomed Chameleon into his house in the forest. Together the god and the lizard shared a flask of palm wine. Then Obatala said, "Tell my master Olorun that I have only two complaints about this new world: it is too cold and it is too dark."

The Chameleon thanked Obatala for his hospitality, then climbed slowly back up the chain. He gave Obatala's message to Olorun and the chief god considered it carefully.

He commanded that there should be made a ball of burning golden light. When it was ready, Olorun took it to the edge of the Sky and hung it there. Light and warmth shone from the ball, down to the earth. It was the sun.

Obatala was so glad to see the sun! His eyes feasted on its beauty and his body basked in its warmth.

But he still had only the black cat to keep him company, and nobody to talk to, so now he had another complaint: he was lonely. He said to himself, "I need people, to surround me with conversation and laughter. I will have to make some."

He took some clay, mixed it with water and formed it into shapes that resembled the gods and goddesses. When each shape was finished, he lay it on the sun to dry, then began to work on another.

On and on Obatala worked, on and on without stopping. This made him hot and thirsty, so he drank many flasks of palm wine. The wine quenched his thirst – but it also made him sleepy and drunk.

Yet still Obatala continued frenziedly working. He made many more clay people, not noticing that some were not properly finished.

In the end Oabatala grew too tired to make any more. He fell into a deep sleep. When he awoke, he called loudly to Olorun, high above in the Sky:

"Master! See all the people I have made! I beg you to bring them to life."

Olorun looked and marvelled at Obatala's creations. He blew the breath of life into them. He turned the clay of their bodies into blood, bones and flesh, and put thoughts into their heads.

The people stood up. They walked and danced. They spoke and sang. They swarmed around Obatala.

The god's heart surged with joy at the sight of his creations. He gave the people hoes for farming and tools for building. The people used the hoes to clear the land and grow crops. They used the building tools to put up many fine houses, turning Obatala's lonely home into the bustling city of Ife.

However, amongst these people,

Obatala suddenly noticed that some could not walk, others could not see, and some were pale and weak with sickness. He remembered how he had been drunk when he created them and his heart swelled with an overwhelming love.

He went to them and said, "Listen. Of all the countless people I made, you are the ones I love most. You are my special people. You must call me whenever you need me, for I will always do my best to protect and help you."

And with these words, Obatala went to his golden chain, climbed up it and returned to his true home in the sky.

Beyond the edge of the earth, in the great sea that still surrounded it, someone had seen him leaving. It was the goddess Olokun, the old ruler of the Water.

Through all Obatala's long work of creation, Olokun had suffered badly. She had lost half of her realm when it was smothered by dry land. She had seen her quiet, grey expanse of emptiness filled with creeping forest and noisy people. Where once there had been watery peace, broken only by the soothing rhythm of the waves, now there was a tangled chaos of human beings and vegetation.

Because of this, Olokun was wild and angry.

So she sang to the waters and made them rise. She called to the air and brought down rain. She was determined to destroy Obatala's land and creation in a flood.

The people felt the rain. They saw the rivers rising, the sea breaking madly over the white beaches, and their land sinking under a deluge of swirling, water-logged mud. They screamed to Obatala for help.

Obatala heard them. He went again to Orunmila and asked him to cast his nuts of wisdom. Again, Orunmila read how the nuts fell in their mysterious patterns. Then he drew upon their powers of healing and

used them to beat down the waves, soothe the swollen rivers and turn back the raging sea.

Since then, the world has been as we know it.

About the people who tell this story

This myth belongs to the Yoruba people, who live in south-western Nigeria in west Africa.

Yoruba civilization goes back at least a thousand years. Their oldest known towns were built at this time. Many of these towns were like mini-kingdoms. One of the most important was the ancient kingdom of Benin. Some of the other towns were joined together to form a powerful empire called Oyo.

Today there are about ten million Yoruba people. About half of them still live in fairly large towns, including the

300-year-old city of Lagos, the biggest in Nigeria. Many others live in villages amongst the tropical forest where farming cacao trees (to produce cocoa) is an important occupation. Ife, mentioned in the myth as the site where Obatala first landed on the earth, has been a major town for over 600 years. Today it is an industrial city, and home to about a quarter of a million people.

The Mud People
A Chinese creation myth

Look:

Everything starts with chaos.

There is swirling confusion, deafening noise, darkness.

Metal, air, fire, water and wood spin through the air. They shatter into tiny fragments, then join together to form...

... an egg.

A huge egg. The first egg.

Time passes. Why hurry? What must

happen, will happen in the end. Eighteen thousand years roll slowly by.

And then...

Inside the egg strange events begin. Shadow melts into light. Coolness mixes with heat. Yin comes together with Yang.

Wait. The egg is ripening.

Suddenly –
it cracks! Then it bursts open. The top floats up, light as dreams, to form the realm of Heaven. The bottom sinks like lead, down, down: it is the Earth. And from the middle there steps out a god.

His name is Pan Gu. He is very small, a

dwarf. He has horns on his head and he wears a cloak of softly rustling leaves.

Pan Gu stretches. He grows taller: three metres taller each day. Many days pass. He pushes Heaven up higher and Earth down lower. Months pass. Years pass. Centuries pass. Still Pan Gu stretches and pushes. Another eighteen thousand years go by.

His work is done. Heaven and Earth are both in place. Pan Gu lies down and dies.

And then... everything shifts and changes. His body crumbles and transforms.

His blood becomes the rivers and seas, realms of the dragon-kings. His flesh becomes the soil, his bones and teeth turn into metal and stone. His breath becomes the wind, his sweat the rain. His left eye is the sun and his right eye the moon. His voice becomes the thunder.

There, it is finished. Heaven and Earth are made.

Who can say how long ago all this happened?

And who can say when it was that gentle Nü Gua came from the towering Kunlun mountains and walked into the world?

This Nü Gua: was she a goddess? Who knows, who can guess the answers to ten thousand mysteries?

Nü Gua roamed through the new-made earth. She saw water flowing down the mountain-sides, trees and flowers growing from the soil, fish swimming in the sea, birds flying in the sky and many animals and insects running, hiding, and crawling across the land.

Nü Gua said to herself, "This is all so beautiful! And yet... why is there an emptiness in my heart? Why do I feel so lonely?"

She went to a pool and gazed into the deep, dark water. Its surface was calm and shimmering, a mirror. In it she saw the sky, the clouds, the wind-swaying reeds at the pool's edge. And... something else. Her own face.

For a long time she gazed at her own reflection. She smiled at it and her heart rose as the reflection smiled back. She waved and was overjoyed to see the friendly gesture returned by the reflection in the water. An idea grew in her mind.

Nü Gua reached out into the pool and scooped up some yellow mud. She moulded the mud with her hands and shaped it, into a copy of herself. When it was finished, she placed it on the ground. At once the mud person transformed and came to life!

It was a woman, the first mortal woman – the first human being in the whole world. She was so happy to find herself alive that she gave a great shout of joy.

So Nü Gua made some more mud people. She made them male and female, tall and short, fat and skinny. As each one came alive it wandered off into the mountains, valleys or forests. From these places Nü Gua heard their laughter. The sound of it made her laugh too.

Now Nü Gua's excitement turned her bold and inventive. She took a long, trailing vine covered in leaves. She dipped it in the watery mud then pulled it out and flicked it through the air. Drops of mud flew everywhere, wildly in the sunshine; and where each one fell to earth it was transformed at once into a person.

Soon Nü Gua had filled the whole world with mud people. They built cities, made paper covered with marvellous

writing, wove silk into flowing dresses, fought in armies led by mighty emperors, celebrated with fireworks.

So everything was ready, and history could begin.

About the people who tell this story

One fifth of all the world's people live in China, which is the third largest country in the world. Its rich civilization goes back over 4,000 years. For most of that time it was ruled by a series of emperors, but during the 20th Century it went through a major revolution that totally changed its way of life.

This myth belongs to the Daoist religion, which teaches people to live in harmony with the ebb and flow of nature. The opposite forces of yin and yang, which are mentioned at the beginning of the story, are a Daoist idea: yin represents the female side of life, and yang is masculine. In traditional Chinese thought, Daoism is often mixed with Buddhism, with Confucianism which teaches a set of moral rules, and with caring for the family ancestors.

Although these religions are not now widely practised in China itself, they are still followed by millions of Chinese people in Hong Kong, Taiwan, Macao and other countries throughout the world.

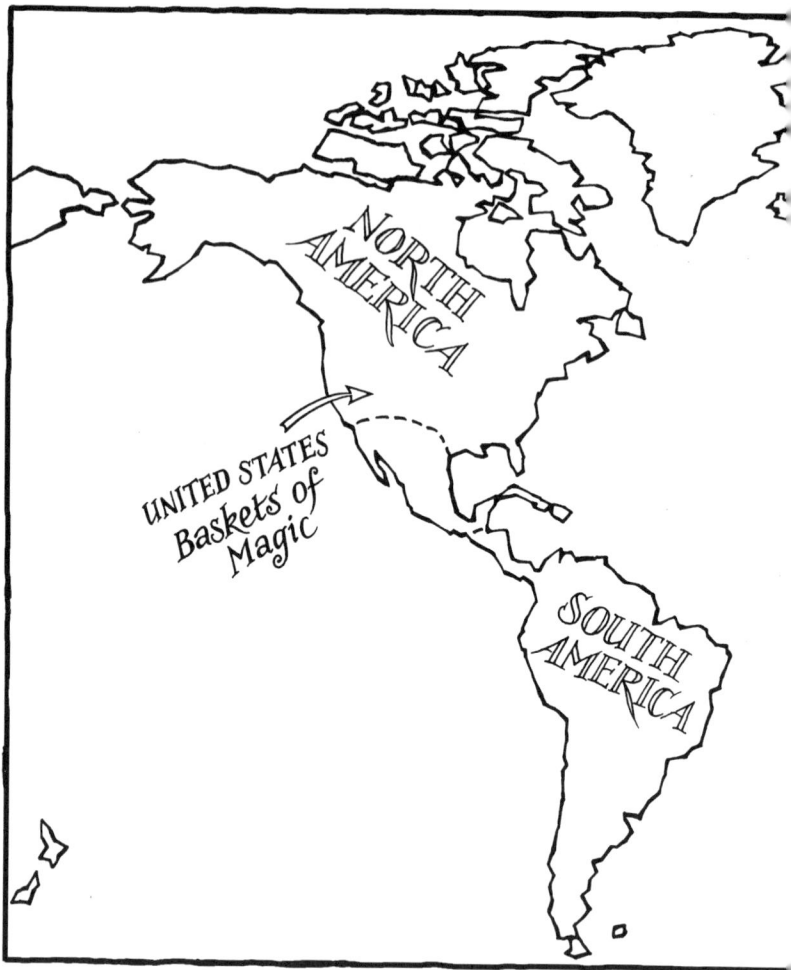

NORTH
AMERICA

UNITED STATES
Baskets of
Magic

SOUTH
AMERICA

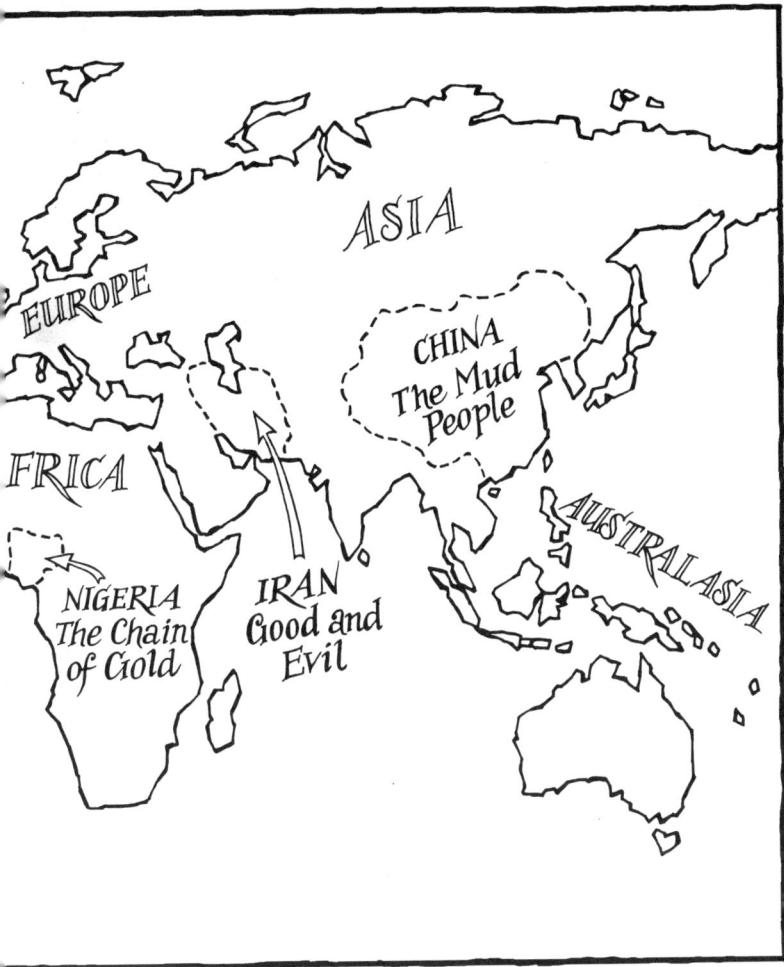

ASIA

EUROPE

CHINA
The Mud
People

AFRICA

AUSTRALASIA

NIGERIA
The Chain
of Gold

IRAN
Good and
Evil

About the author

I've written over fifty books – mostly for children, but also a few for teachers. Some of these have been translated into many different languages, ranging from Icelandic to Japanese!

I especially enjoy telling traditional stories: myths, legends and folk tales. It gives me a haunting feeling to be directly linked to the great story-tellers of long ago. On my shelves at home I have hundreds of books of traditional stories from all over the world. I collect them in the way that other people collect stamps. I simply can't resist their wonderful mix of strange adventure and magic.